CGP has Handwriting sorted all autumn!

It's crucial to keep working on Handwriting skills throughout Year 4, and this CGP book is a brilliant way to keep pupils practising regularly...

It's packed with fun, engaging exercises for every day of the autumn term, covering all the words they'll need to use most often.

We've included plenty of full sentences and paragraphs to tackle too — perfect for helping them build up their fluency and confidence!

What CGP is all about

Our sole aim here at CGP is to produce the highest quality books — carefully written, immaculately presented and dangerously close to being funny.

Then we work our socks off to get them out to you — at the cheapest possible prices.

Contents

☑ Use the tick boxes to help keep a record of which pages have been attempted.

Week 1
- ☑ Day 1 1
- ☑ Day 2 2
- ☑ Day 3 3
- ☑ Day 4 4
- ☑ Day 5 5

Week 2
- ☑ Day 1 6
- ☑ Day 2 7
- ☑ Day 3 8
- ☑ Day 4 9
- ☑ Day 5 10

Week 3
- ☑ Day 1 11
- ☑ Day 2 12
- ☑ Day 3 13
- ☑ Day 4 14
- ☑ Day 5 15

Week 4
- ☑ Day 1 16
- ☑ Day 2 17
- ☑ Day 3 18
- ☑ Day 4 19
- ☑ Day 5 20

Week 5
- ☑ Day 1 21
- ☑ Day 2 22
- ☑ Day 3 23
- ☑ Day 4 24
- ☑ Day 5 25

Week 6
- ☑ Day 1 26
- ☑ Day 2 27
- ☑ Day 3 28
- ☑ Day 4 29
- ☑ Day 5 30

Week 7
- ☑ Day 1 31
- ☑ Day 2 32
- ☑ Day 3 33
- ☑ Day 4 34
- ☑ Day 5 35

Week 8
- ☑ Day 1 36
- ☑ Day 2 37
- ☑ Day 3 38
- ☑ Day 4 39
- ☑ Day 5 40

Week 9

- [✓] Day 1 41
- [✓] Day 2 42
- [✓] Day 3 43
- [✓] Day 4 44
- [✓] Day 5 45

Week 10

- [✓] Day 1 46
- [✓] Day 2 47
- [✓] Day 3 48
- [✓] Day 4 49
- [✓] Day 5 50

Week 11

- [✓] Day 1 51
- [✓] Day 2 52
- [✓] Day 3 53
- [✓] Day 4 54
- [✓] Day 5 55

Week 12

- [✓] Day 1 56
- [✓] Day 2 57
- [✓] Day 3 58
- [✓] Day 4 59
- [✓] Day 5 60

Published by CGP

ISBN: 978 1 78908 664 5

Editors: Rachel Craig-McFeely, Mary Falkner, Rob Hayman, Sharon Keeley-Holden and Camilla Sheridan.

With thanks to Alison Griffin and Hayley Thompson for the proofreading.
With thanks to Emily Smith for the copyright research.

Printed by Elanders Ltd, Newcastle upon Tyne.
Clipart on the cover and throughout the book from Corel®
Images used on pages 2, 10 and 20 © www.edu-clips.com
Based on the classic CGP style created by Richard Parsons.

Text, design, layout and original illustrations © Coordination Group Publications Ltd. (CGP) 2020
All rights reserved.

Photocopying this book is not permitted, even if you have a CLA licence.
Extra copies are available from CGP with next day delivery • 0800 1712 712 • www.cgpbooks.co.uk

How to Use this Book

- This book contains 60 pages of daily handwriting practice.

- It's split into 12 sections — that's roughly one section for each week of the Year 4 Autumn term.

- A week is made up of 5 pages, so there's one for every school day of the term (Monday – Friday).

- Each page should take about 10 minutes to complete.

- Each week, pupils practise copying individual words, such as spelling words from the National Curriculum, then whole sentences and paragraphs with a particular theme. This helps them to build up their handwriting fluency.

- A typical page looks something like this:

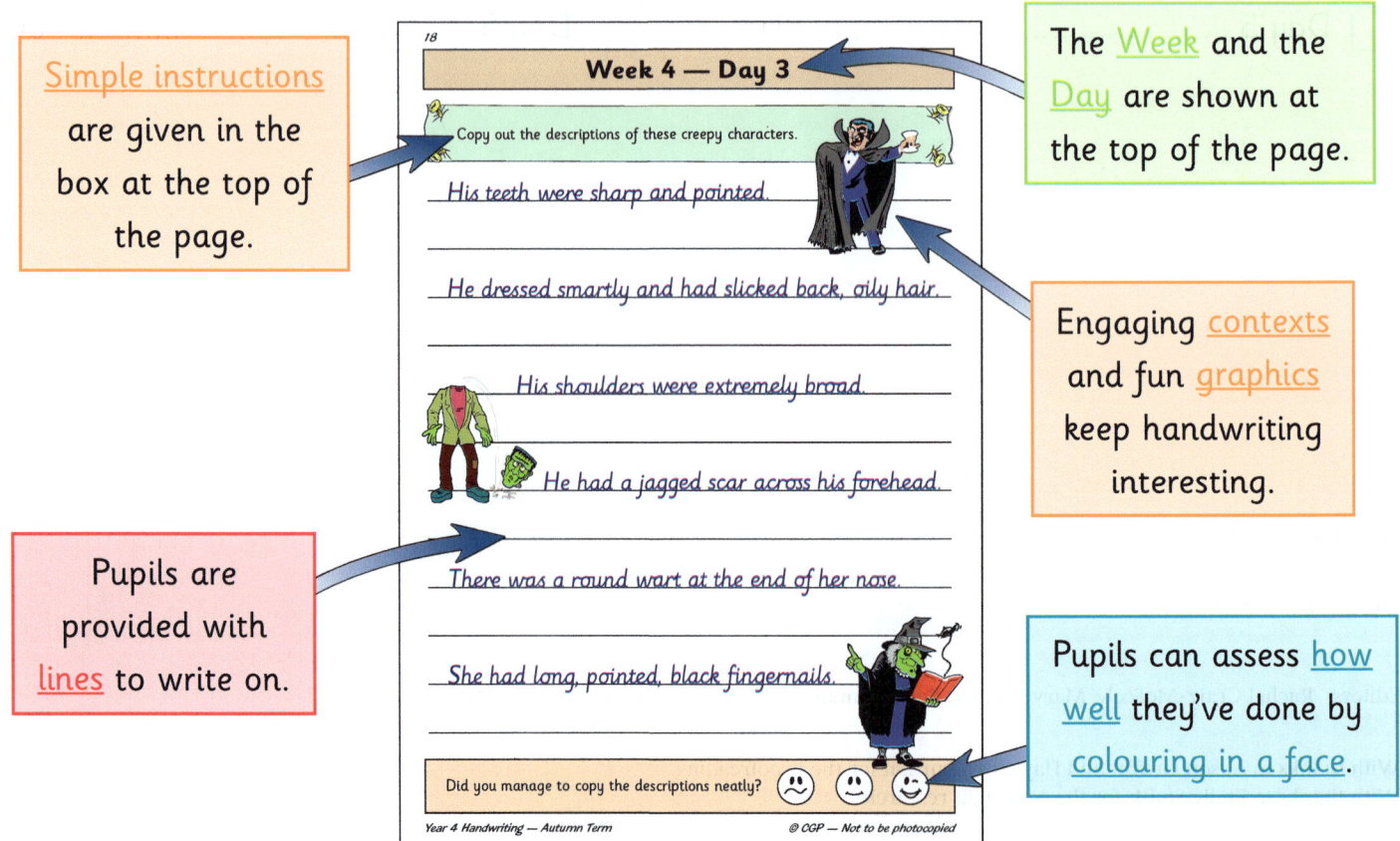

If you are a parent or guardian using this book at home with your child, you should bear in mind that different schools have different handwriting styles. You should check with the school to see how they write and join each letter. Some schools also have different break letters (letters that don't join to the next letter). For example, 'g' can be a break letter or can be joined. You should check which break letters the school uses.

Week 1 — Day 1

Copy each of these words three times across the page.

accident

accidental

actual

actually

address

answer

appear

arrive

believe

bicycle

breath

breathe

How well do you believe you did today?

Week 1 — Day 2

 Carefully copy each of these sentences on the line underneath.

The squirrel carrying the nut swiftly climbed the tree.

_____

A breeze rustled the leaves in the ancient wood.

_____

Beneath the squirrel, a deer relaxed in the shade.

_____

 Cautiously, the squirrel crept along a thin branch.

_____

He heaved the smooth, shiny nut onto his shoulder.

_____

The cheeky squirrel aimed the nut at the deer.

_____

 How did you manage with this page?

Week 1 — Day 3

Copy each of these fascinating facts about sloths.

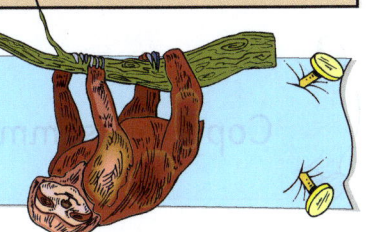

Sloths are found in South and Central America.

Their really long claws make walking difficult.

Sloths spend their time hanging from branches.

Munching leaves as they go, they move very slowly.

Although they are slow climbers, they can swim fast.

Once a week, they leave the trees to go to the toilet.

How neatly did you copy these facts?

Week 1 — Day 4

Copy this summary of a Greek myth neatly.

Icarus and Daedalus were imprisoned in a tower. To escape, Daedalus made wings out of wax and feathers. He warned Icarus not to fly too high as the sun would melt the wax, but Icarus forgot the warning. He flew so high that his wings came apart and he fell into the sea and drowned.

How well did you manage to copy this story?

Week 1 — Day 5

Susie wrote a postcard to her friend about a dramatic event. Copy what she wrote below.

To my dear friend Mohammad,
I'm having a great time in Skegness. However, I must tell you about an alarming incident on the beach yesterday. The donkey I was riding galloped off at a furious pace. She left the beach and raced to a greengrocers. She must have smelled carrots!

How neatly did you copy the postcard?

Week 2 — Day 1

Copy out each of the words three times.

caught

business

build

calendar

certain

complete

century

busy

continue

centre

circle

consider

How well did you manage to write these words?

Week 2 — Day 2

Copy out these examples of direct speech.

"Red card!" barked the referee.

Yashvi asked, "How much is this please?"

I yelled, "Be careful!" as Gran sped off.

"Get on with your work!" shouted Mr Cadell.

"It's so sunny today," said Kaye, happily.

The astronaut whispered, "He's seen us."

Were you able to copy these sentences neatly?

Week 2 — Day 3

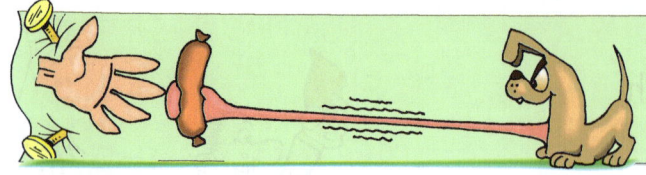 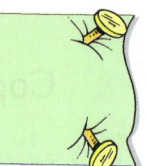

Copy out these sentences.

He said the dog took the sausage out of his hand.

James asked if there were any more pancakes left.

In his sternest voice, Dad ordered us to go to bed.

I told them that I had never seen so much snow.

Lucy said that she prefers baths to showers because she can sit in them for ten hours.

How did you get on with these sentences?

Week 2 — Day 4

This paragraph sets the scene for a story. Copy it out on the lines below.

The bare, cracked landscape stretched endlessly. A bird circling high above was the only sign of movement. Off the dusty track up ahead were the remains of crumbling buildings, heat scorched paint peeling from their doors and tatty shutters hanging from a single hinge. This town was long forgotten.

How did this page go?

Week 2 — Day 5

Copy this riddle out below.

I have rivers and oceans, yet no water or fish.
I have countries and borders, but you may travel as you wish.
My surface is smooth, not a bump to be seen.
I am mainly blue, but the rest of me is green.
What am I?

I'm a globe (or a world map)!

Did you copy the riddle out neatly?

Week 3 — Day 1

Copy out each of the words below three times.

decide

describe

different

difficult

disappear

early

earth

eight

eighth

enough

exercise

experience

Did you copy all of these words excellently?

Week 3 — Day 2

Copy out the sentences below.

Rex has eaten too much ice cream.

Ama has read all the books in the library.

She has slipped on a banana peel.

I am excited because it has snowed all day.

When you've finished your work, you can go.

Ali has won a cheese-eating competition.

Have you copied out these sentences neatly?

Week 3 — Day 3

Have a go at copying out the story openings below.

The door slammed shut. I was trapped.

Ella wasn't like the other witches.

She started to run, gasping at the icy winter air.

The moon shone eerily over the deserted house.

Everything changed the day the aliens arrived.

Saul was seven when he saw the first ghost.

Did you copy out these story openings well?

Week 3 — Day 4

Have a go at copying out this limerick.

There is a Young Lady whose nose

Continually prospers and grows;

When it grew out of sight,

She exclaimed in a fright,

"Oh! Farewell to the end of my nose!"

by Edward Lear

How did you get on with this limerick?

Week 3 — Day 5

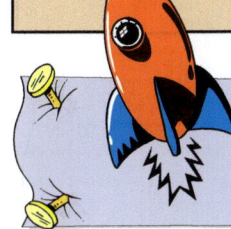

Copy this job advert on the lines below.

Amazing astronaut wanted!

Are you fascinated by space?

Do you want to visit other galaxies?

Would you like to fly a rocket?

If you have answered yes to all these questions, apply today! Do you have what it takes?

Was your handwriting out of this world?

Week 4 — Day 1

Copy out the twelve words below three times.

experiment

extreme

famous

favourite

February

forwards

fruit

grammar

group

guard

guide

heard

How did you find writing out these words?

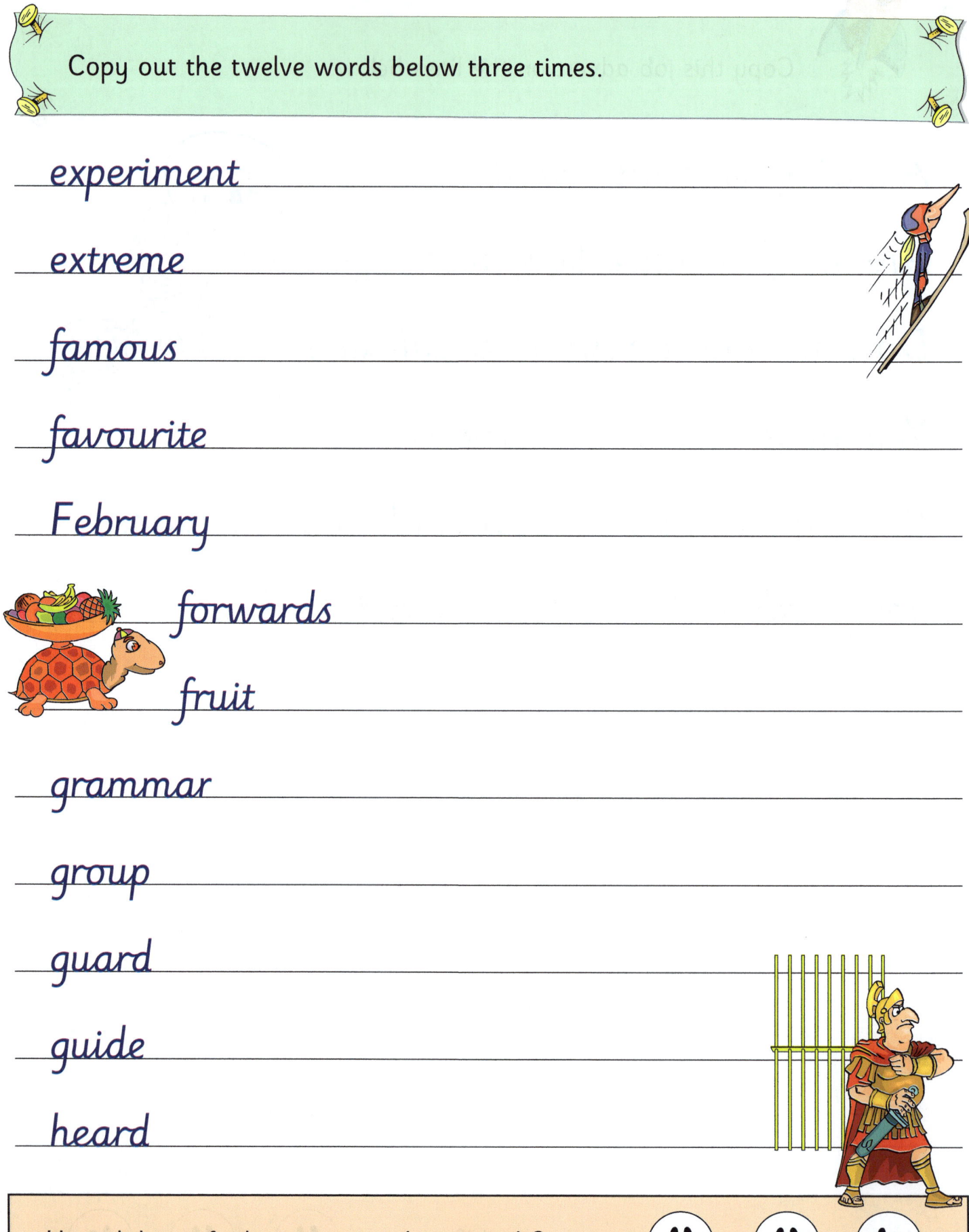

Week 4 — Day 2

Copy the sentences below.
They show how pronouns can be used.

Kat ran the marathon. She trained very hard for it.

Rob loves cheese on toast. It is his favourite meal.

Amit hopes his next football will last him longer.

Julia lives in York. She prefers it to London.

Ed has two cats. They are called Alfie and Rupert.

Hati climbs twice a week. It keeps her fit.

How did you get on with these sentences?

Week 4 — Day 3

Copy out the descriptions of these creepy characters.

His teeth were sharp and pointed.

He dressed smartly and had slicked back, oily hair.

His shoulders were extremely broad.

He had a jagged scar across his forehead.

There was a round wart at the end of her nose.

She had long, pointed, black fingernails.

Did you manage to copy the descriptions neatly?

Week 4 — Day 4

This paragraph describes how some fossils are formed. Read the paragraph and then copy it out.

Plants and animals die and sink to the bottom of the sea. Their soft parts decompose, leaving behind hard parts, like bones. These get buried in layers of sand and mud, which turn to rock over millions of years. Eventually, the hard parts dissolve leaving a shape in the rock which is a fossil.

Did you make a neat copy of the paragraph?

Week 4 — Day 5

Copy out this piece of writing, which tries to persuade the reader to use fewer plastic water bottles.

How many plastic bottles do you think are used in the UK each year? Go on, guess... Over 7 billion! It really is shocking, isn't it? But don't worry, you can make a huge difference with one small, simple step. Just bring your own water bottle when you go on a day out and refill it. It couldn't be easier!

Did you manage to copy the paragraph neatly?

Week 5 — Day 1

Copy each of these words out three times.

heart

height

history

imagine

increase

important

interest

island

knowledge

learn

length

library

How did you find copying out these words?

Week 5 — Day 2

Copy out these sentences. They all contain connecting words.

Hamish ran away when he saw the spider.

The pig ate the apples until it was full.

After Kelly licked the ice lolly, her tongue was cold.

 Patch was clean before she rolled in the mud.

While Jim was fishing, Suzi saw a massive shark.

Once the spider disappeared, Hamish came outside.

How well did you do with today's sentences?

Week 5 — Day 3

Have a go at copying out the sentences below.

Clara adopted a dog even though Ali prefers cats.

We flew to Spain because Wales can be drizzly.

Mum was at work, so we ate chocolate for lunch.

I wanted to play in the sun, but the teacher said no.

Yuri created an imaginary friend who kept eating all of the biscuits.

How do you think you did with these sentences?

Week 5 — Day 4

Copy out these sentences about a Viking god.

Thursday is named after Thor.

Thor is the Norse god of thunder and lightning.

His mother was a giant.

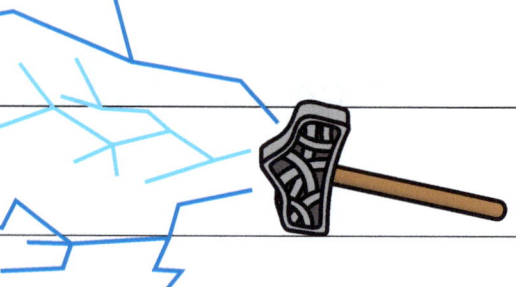

He smashes enemies with a hammer called Mjölnir.

He rides in a chariot pulled by two goats.

He once fought a snake the size of the world.

Were you able to write these sentences correctly?

Week 5 — Day 5

Copy out this advert for a holiday camp.

Come and stay at Sandy Sun Holiday Camp!

Take advantage of our tremendous beach.

Every meal comes with two free flies.

The water in our pool is a unique shade of brown.

We promise that your sheets were washed last year.

Just ignore the mysterious creature in the wardrobe.

How was your handwriting today?

Week 6 — Day 1

Copy each of these wonderful words three times.

material

medicine

mention

minute

natural

naughty

notice

occasion

occasional

often

opposite

ordinary

How neatly did you copy these words?

Week 6 — Day 2

Copy each sentence on the line below.

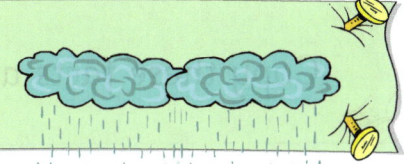

Even if it rains, we're off to the beach.

I am really hungry because I forgot to bring lunch.

Holly weighed the flour whilst Joe cracked the eggs.

I really don't like jelly as it is far too wobbly.

After arriving at the beach, Max bought a balloon.

I get brain freeze when I eat ice cream.

How did you get on with these sentences?

Week 6 — Day 3

Copy these facts about the planets of our Solar System.

There are eight planets in the Solar System.

Jupiter, the largest planet, is a giant ball of gas.

 This means it has no solid surface.

Jupiter's red spot is actually a raging storm.

Saturn is a gas planet which has spectacular rings.

These are made of ice and rock.

How neatly did you copy these fascinating facts?

Week 6 — Day 4

As neatly as you can, copy this paragraph.

The International Space Station orbits the Earth sixteen times a day. It was taken to space piece by piece and assembled by astronauts. The people living on it float around weightlessly. There are labs where they do experiments and also six sleeping cabins, two bathrooms and a gym.

How did you get on with this paragraph?

Week 6 — Day 5

Copy this account of what it might be like to wake up on board the International Space Station.

I awoke in my sleeping bag, which was clipped to the wall. If it hadn't been, I would have been floating around all night bumping into things. First, I had a wash using tiny amounts of water and liquid soap. Next, I brushed my teeth, keeping my mouth shut to stop the toothpaste escaping.

How neat was your writing?

Week 7 — Day 1

Copy out the twelve words below three times.

particular

peculiar

perhaps

popular

position

possess

possession

possible

potatoes

pressure

probably

promise

Could you copy these words perfectly?

Week 7 — Day 2

Copy out these sentences, which contain prepositions that show when or why something happens.

Ron hid while Tina closed her eyes and counted.

After one minute, Tina started her search.

Due to Ron's brilliant hiding, Tina couldn't find him anywhere and soon gave up.

Ron kept hiding during tea. When he finally came out, Tina laughed until she cried.

Did you write the sentences neatly on the lines?

Week 7 — Day 3

Have a go at copying out the proverbs (well-known sayings) below.

Every cloud has a silver lining.

A bad workman always blames his tools.

Actions speak louder than words.

A leopard can't change its spots.

An apple a day keeps the doctor away.

Don't judge a book by its cover.

Were your proverbs copied correctly?

Week 7 — Day 4

Read this text, taken from a spooky story. Then, copy it out below.

A full moon shone over the village, lighting up the faces of the children who ran from house to house, gathering sweets. However, the children were not the only ones enjoying the evening. Tonight was the night that the monsters came out to play...

Was your handwriting scarily good?

Week 7 — Day 5

Read the instructions on how to make a magic potion. Can you copy them on the lines below?

First, boil some dew in a cauldron.

Next, add two spoonfuls of frog slime, a jar of spiders and a dash of powdered unicorn horn.

Stir the mixture carefully using a magic wand.

Then, add a small sprinkle of ancient stardust.

Your invisibility potion is complete! Use it wisely.

Could you copy these sentences as if by magic?

Week 8 — Day 1

Copy out each of these words three times.

purpose

quarter

question

recent

regular

reign

remember

sentence

separate

special

straight

strange

Did you neatly copy all of these words?

Week 8 — Day 2

Write out each of these sentences below.

Unexpectedly, Asisat's flowers had grown.

Out of breath, Polly stumbled over the finish line.

Every year, Vikram buys a brand new hat.

Hungrily, the tiger leapt out of the undergrowth.

Deep in the forest, Hugo found a haunted castle.

Under the sea, you'll find Jake's treasure.

How did you get on with these sentences?

Week 8 — Day 3

Read and then copy out these facts about light.

Sources of light, such as the Sun, give out light.

 Light always travels in straight lines.

Light is the fastest thing in the entire Universe.

When light is blocked, you get a shadow.

Shiny surfaces reflect lots of light.

Looking at a bright light can damage your eyes.

How did you do with these facts?

Week 8 — Day 4

This page contains an extract from a poem. Copy it out.

From "My Shadow" by Robert Louis Stevenson

I have a little shadow that goes in and out with me,

And what can be the use of him is more than I can see.

He is very, very like me

from the heels up to the head;

And I see him jump before me, when I jump into my bed.

How does your copied poem look?

Week 8 — Day 5

Copy out this paragraph about the Ancient Greek god Apollo.

Apollo was the god of light in Greek mythology.

He was also the god of music, poetry and medicine.

He lived with eleven other gods

at the top of Mount Olympus.

At his shrine in Delphi, Apollo would tell people

the future through a priestess called the Oracle.

Did you copy this paragraph neatly?

Week 9 — Day 1

Copy each of these words out three times.

strength

suppose

surprise

therefore

though

although

thought

through

various

weight

woman

women

Did you copy out each of the words neatly?

Week 9 — Day 2

All of these sentences contain possessive apostrophes. Carefully copy out each sentence.

Lyn's serve was incredibly powerful.

The sheriff's golden badge glistened in the sunlight.

Charles's curries and stews are always delicious.

The boxer's gloves were too big for him.

My brothers' names are Bruce, Bryn and Bryan.

Tennis and karate are Kie's favourite sports.

How did you get on with copying these sentences?

Week 9 — Day 3

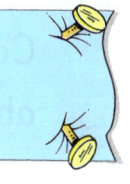

Copy out these sentences about winter.

In winter, the temperature can get very low.

Unless I wear socks, my toes freeze when I'm in bed!

Some animals, like bats, hibernate over winter.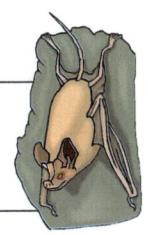

It gets dark much earlier in the evening.

I have to wrap up warm when I play outside.

We drink hot chocolate and warm up by the fire.

Brrrr! How did you do?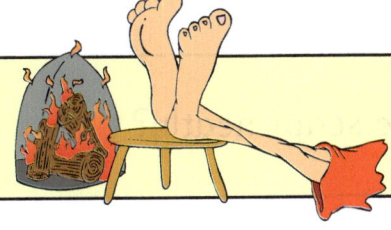

Week 9 — Day 4

Copy out this extract of a script. It's from a play about a magician whose trick works too well...

A magician stands behind the closed stage curtain of a packed theatre. His assistant enters hurriedly.

Week 9 — Day 5

Copy out this paragraph describing a type of mythical creature called a Boggart.

If you're from the north of England you might have heard of a Boggart, or even have your own. These mischievous spirits love playing irritating pranks. Their favourites include making milk go sour and stealing one sock from a pair. So, be warned, if you keep losing your keys, there may be more to it...

How did you get on with this paragraph?

Week 10 — Day 1

These words all contain prefixes.
Copy them out three times.

disappoint

disbelief

disordered

disgrace

inactive

incapable

incorrect

independent

misbehave

mislead

misplace

misspell

Were your words and prefixes practically perfect?

Week 10 — Day 2

 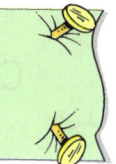

These sentences use some words that you've practised earlier on in this book. Copy them out neatly.

Sadiq was certain that he had walked in a circle.

Lola is able to hold her breath for eight minutes.

King Ed's reign lasted for over a century.

"Exercise is the best medicine," said Jan.

 *Princess Rosie was guided by her heart.*

 *At wizard school they learn difficult spells.*

How well did you copy out the sentences?

Week 10 — Day 3

Copy out these amazing facts about the rainforest.

Rainforests get at least 250 cm of rain a year.

The climate is usually warm and humid.

Chocolate and coffee come from the rainforest.

Millions of animal species inhabit rainforests.

The Amazon rainforest is the largest rainforest in the world. It is almost twice the size of India.

Could you copy these facts fabulously?

Week 10 — Day 4

Read this description of the Amazon rainforest, then copy it out below.

Despite the deep shade, the air is hot and sticky, rich with the smell of damp plants. Huge trees grow high into the sky, topped with a thick canopy of leaves. The air is filled with a chorus of buzzing, howling and bird song. Birds flash past as monkeys swing high above.

Did you copy out the description neatly?

Week 10 — Day 5

Here is a recipe for toad in the hole.
Read the instructions, then copy them out.

Cook some sausages in a large tray. Meanwhile, make a batter by mixing flour with eggs and milk. Whisk the batter until it is smooth. Take the tray of sausages out of the oven and pour in the batter. Cook for half an hour until the batter has risen. Serve with gravy.

Was your handwriting as great as this recipe?

Week 11 — Day 1

These words contain prefixes. Copy them out three times.

illegal

illegible

immature

immortal

impatient

impossible

irregular

irrelevant

irrational

refresh

 return

redecorate

How well did you copy these words?

Week 11 — Day 2

The sentences below contain some words that you practised earlier on in this book. Have a go at copying them out on the lines below.

Tom accidentally fell off his bicycle.

Carrie is famous for her extreme strength.

The mischievous dog licked his lips.

The guard promised to watch the fruit carefully.

Ghosts are often heard in the haunted house.

I thought that the potatoes looked peculiar.

Did you write the sentences neatly?

Week 11 — Day 3

Read these facts about Grace Darling, then copy them out underneath.

Grace Darling was born in 1815.

Grace lived in a lighthouse by the sea.

She saw a ship being wrecked in a terrible storm.

Grace and her father risked their lives to row to the shipwreck and rescue the survivors.

Grace became famous for her bravery.

Did you copy out these facts fantastically?

Week 11 — Day 4

Here is a description of a storm at sea. Copy it out on the lines below.

Storm clouds hang heavily over the rough waves. The sea is transformed into a wild, boiling beast by the howling wind. Suddenly the rain begins, erupting from the clouds like ash from a volcano. The black sky is lit up by lightning as the thunder roars angrily.

How did you get on with copying the description?

Week 11 — Day 5

Here is a diary entry that could have been written by Grace Darling. Copy it out neatly.

Dear diary, today was the scariest day of my life. Last night, there was an awful storm and a ship struck the rocks. Father and I decided to try to save the survivors. Rowing our tiny boat through the huge waves was the hardest thing I have ever done, but it was worth it — we saved nine people.

Were you a handwriting hero on this page?

Week 12 — Day 1

All of these words start with a prefix. Copy each word out twice.

interact

antiseptic

superhuman

autograph

subheading

subdivide

international

supermarket

autobiography

anticlockwise

intercity

submerge

Was your handwriting super?

Week 12 — Day 2

Read these sentences and then copy them out below.

February was missing from Marcel's calendar.

Lise's recent experiments had exploded.

Surprisingly, dolphins cannot breathe underwater.

Alfie ran straight for his favourite toy.

It is possible for a giraffe's height to be five metres.

"Eight cakes was probably too many," groaned Ivy.

Did you write all of these sentences neatly?

Week 12 — Day 3

Here are five Christmas traditions from around the world. Copy each one out neatly on the lines below.

Japanese families share fried chicken.

In Venezuela, people roller skate to church.

Ukrainians decorate their trees with spider webs.

Danish people eat rice pudding on Christmas Eve.

In Iceland, people wear new clothes to scare off a monster called the "Yule Cat".

How did you find writing these sentences?

Week 12 — Day 4

This is part of a poem is by Clement Clarke Moore. Copy out each line on the lines below.

'Twas the night before Christmas,

when all through the house

Not a creature was stirring,

not even a mouse;

The stockings were hung by the chimney with care,

In hopes that St. Nicholas soon would be there.

Did you manage to copy the lines neatly?

Week 12 — Day 5

Here are three Christmas jokes for you to copy out. Merry Christmas!

What do Santa's teachers give out at school?

Ho Ho Homework!

What do snowmen eat for their breakfast?

Snow Flakes!

What do you call a cat dressed as Santa?

Santa Paws!

Have you neatly copied these hilarious jokes?

Year 4 Handwriting — Autumn Term